through our eyes

An anthology

Tales of culture and tradition
–for kids, by kids

Aditi Wardhan Singh
COACH AND EDITOR

dedication

This book is an ode to dreamers, writers, and creators...

This is book two in the Through Our Eyes Anthologies. This series was created to empower kids who dream of becoming authors and creators. To provide them the tools through hands-on guidance and comprehensive coaching to get a real behind the scenes of being a published author.

Every story here is born of our yearly Write to Publish Program.

The prompt: Show your culture, traditions or festivals in a new light. The kids took up the challenge and how! With gentle guidance, these kids have written quality stories that showcase how storytelling is a wonderful way to share one's culture and their sense of self. While reading this story, you are bound to find yourself not only enlightened but also will get a peek into the creative mind of a young author.

Contents

Chapter 1

The Magical Experience

Arjun Patel was the bravest man in the whole town. He lived in a small shack on top of a rocky hill. He had sharp black eyes that looked like they could see through anything. A scar ran across his cheek from when he fought a tiger, and people said his hands looked rough from climbing mountains. Kids whispered about his adventures, and everyone thought he was a hero. Arjun liked being brave, but sometimes he also liked taking risks that made other people nervous.

He never went on adventures alone. His little sister Mira always followed him. She had long black hair in a braid and kind brown eyes. Mira worried a lot, but she was also really smart and quick. Arjun's best friend Dev always came too. Dev was short, had a loud laugh, and sometimes got scared easily, but he never left Arjun's side. The three of them made a team, even if they argued sometimes.

One morning, Arjun told them he wanted to find the Lost Trident, a powerful weapon from the gods. Mira gasped and told him it belonged to the ocean god, Varuna. She said it was dangerous, but Arjun just grinned and said that's why he wanted it. Dev groaned and muttered that this was a terrible idea, but of course he still followed. Deep down, they were all scared, but they stuck together because that's what friends and family do.

Their first challenge was a dark tunnel. It stretched forever, and water dripped down the stone walls. Shadows made Mira shiver, and Dev jumped at every sound. Arjun held up a torch and walked like nothing could scare him, even though his own heart was beating fast. He never wanted to look afraid because he knew Mira and Dev needed him to be strong. Slowly, they made it through the tunnel together.

Next, they had to cross broken bridges hanging over a huge pit. The wood creaked loudly, and Mira's knees shook so badly she almost froze in the middle.

Arjun grabbed her hand and told her he wouldn't let her fall. Dev crossed last, mumbling prayers the whole time. When he finally made it across, he collapsed on the ground. They laughed nervously, but really, they were just happy to still be alive.

After that, they came to cliffs filled with fire and lava. Sparks shot into the air, and the heat made them sweat. Mira felt dizzy, and Dev looked like he was about to faint. Arjun stayed calm and told them to take it one step at a time. His steady voice helped, and little by little they crossed safely. When they made it to the other side, they felt proud of themselves.

At last, they saw the Trident. It was glowing gold and covered with carvings that looked magical. The air felt heavy, and Arjun's chest pounded as he grabbed it. But then the ground split, and they fell into the ocean below! They landed in a magical underwater world with coral towers and glowing fish swimming past them. Everything sparkled like it was made of gems.

Suddenly, the sea shook and Varuna, the ocean god, appeared. He was huge and glowing like the moon, and his voice rumbled like thunder. "Who dares to take my Trident?" he boomed. Dev hid behind Mira, who stammered, "We didn't mean to upset you." But Arjun stood tall and shouted, "I challenge you, Varuna! If I win, the Trident is mine!" Mira gasped and begged him not to, but Varuna agreed.

The next day, the battle began in an underwater arena filled with sea creatures. The sand glittered, and the water felt heavy. Arjun fought bravely, dodging Varuna's powerful strikes, but the god was too strong. Waves knocked Arjun down again and again until he was weak and bruised. Still, he refused to give up, even when it hurt. That's when Mira shouted, "Arjun, you don't need to win to be brave! You already are!"

Her words made Arjun realize the truth. He dropped to his knees and said, "I give up." The whole arena went quiet. Varuna looked at him for a long time and then smiled. "You are brave," Varuna said, "but bravery without wisdom is dangerous." He put the Trident back in its place, and the three friends floated safely back to the surface.

When they returned home, Arjun looked at Mira and Dev and said softly, "Without you, I would've been lost." Mira smiled, and Dev laughed nervously like he always did. The three of them sat together, tired but safe. From then on, Arjun still wanted adventures, but he knew true bravery meant listening, not just fighting. And deep in the ocean, Varuna guarded the Trident forever.

ABOUT THE AUTHOR

Dilan Patel is 10 years old and enjoys playing soccer, doing Bollywood dance, building new things and being creative. He dreams of becoming a pilot because he loves planes. To all the kids reading this, some advice is to always put your head into the right mindset even if it may be difficult.

Chapter 2

The Voice Against Silence

Nima Patel loved Navratri more than any other time of year. For nine nights, her quiet village near Bhuj, Gujarat, turned bright and busy.

Houses glowed with little oil lamps called diyas. The air smelled like marigold flowers and sweet jalebi frying in hot ghee. Women wore bright chaniya cholis with shiny mirrors that sparkled under the lights. Men wore colorful kediyus and turbans. The dhol drums boomed like thunder. The sound of manjira bells and ghungroos filled the air. Everyone danced Garba and Dandiya Raas in big circles. Nima was sixteen.

At home, life was strict. "Girls should be helpful, not loud," her father often said. But Nima loved to sing. She sang while sweeping, while washing dishes, and even while stirring dal with a wooden spoon like it was a microphone.

Her biggest dream was to sing in Bollywood movies like Lata Mangeshkar or Shreya Ghoshal. Only her best friend Riya knew this secret. On the third night of Navratri, Nima wore her favorite purple chaniya choli. She tied her braid with jasmine flowers that smelled sweet. The temple yard glowed with lights. People clapped to the beat, their feet moving in quick steps. Then the DJ played a Bollywood Garba remix, without thinking, Nima began to sing.

Her voice rose above the drums and bells. People slowed down and turned to listen.

"You sound amazing," Riya whispered.

Nima didn't notice that Riya had her phone out recording her. On the eighth night of Navratri, Riya posted the video online.

The title said: "Village Girl Sings Like a Bollywood Star, Navratri Special!"

The next morning, Nima was carrying laundry and holding down her dupatta in the wind when Riya showed her the phone. Thousands of people had watched the video.

Her cousin Priya ran in. "Everyone's talking about you! Someone in town showed me your video!"

Her father overheard. "What video?" he asked.

When Riya explained, his face grew serious. "Take it down. Our family has a reputation. Girls should not sing for strangers."

That night was the last night of Navratri. The biggest night. The music was faster, and women's skirts spun like flowers. At first, Nima stayed at the edge of the circle. But when the drums got louder, her heart couldn't resist.

She stepped forward, spun, and sang with all her heart. When the dance ended, a man in a black shirt came over.

"Are you Nima Patel? I work at a music company in Ahmedabad. We saw your video. We'd like you to come for an audition."

Her father looked ready to say no, but Nima spoke first. "Thank you. I would love to come!"

A week later, Nima stood in a recording studio. She closed her eyes and imagined the lights of Navratri, the smell of jasmine, and the beat of the dhol. Then she began to sing. Months later, on another Navratri night, Nima stood on a big stage in Mumbai. The crowd clapped and cheered her name.

She smiled, remembering the girl who once sang quietly in the kitchen. Now the whole world was listening and Nima knew she would never be silent again.

ABOUT THE AUTHOR

Diya Patel is 12 years old and enjoys singing, dancing, and soccer. She dreams of becoming a doctor to follow her dad's footsteps. She wants all kids to follow their dreams even if someone tells them they can't do it.

Chapter 3

Hibiscus

Aadi ran around the field, and volleyed the ball into the net. GOAL! He was practicing hard, training for the biggest soccer tournament, the Michigan State Cup. He was prepared to win that trophy.

He kept training in his yard, until his little sister, Kavya, called him for dinner.

Dinner was Puran Poli, a Maharashtrian delicacy made of lentils and jaggery. Aadi was surprised, and wondered what the occasion was. His dad responded, "Aadi, do you know how we go to Ann Arbor every year for the Ganpati celebration?"

"Yes...?" replied Aadi.

"Well, this year we're planning something different. It's a surprise, though."

"Ok! And…?"

"It'll be on the same weekend as your big soccer tournament."

"So, I'll have to miss it?" asked Aadi, dread creeping up his spine. His mom looked down at her lap.

"Yes." said Aadi's dad in a soft tone.

In the upcoming weeks to when he would've been going to the Michigan State Cup, all he could think about was how much he was missing out on, knowing that he had to give up his dream of winning the Championship, and go to a Ganpati festival. He kept playing soccer, hoping that it might cure his chronic FOMO. Of course, it didn't. All of his teammates were going to be there, having the time of their lives in the biggest soccer tournament in the state, and meanwhile, he was going to be stuck at some traditional Ganpati festival. His despair couldn't be cured that easily.

On the day of the flight, Aadi texted all his teammates, wishing them well, and making it clear how much he wanted to go. He felt helpless. He wondered if Ganpati had ever played soccer, and if so, did he ever have to miss a tournament for his own festival?

When they reached the house, his mom grew up in, he ran and hugged his Aaji, or grandma. Aadi looked at her, forlorn, and asked her if Ganpati had ever played soccer, and she responded with a story.

"When Shiva and Parvati offered a divine fruit to whichever of their sons could circle the world three times, Kartikeya sped off on his peacock. Ganesha, riding a slow mouse, simply walked around his parents and said, "You are my world." Touched by his insight and devotion, they awarded him the fruit.

When Kartikeya returned, dusty and tired, he saw Ganpati playing soccer with some other kids, he couldn't help but smile. His brother had won the prize using only wit and love."

That night, in his dreams, Aadi imagined his soccer team losing without him, and guilting him for not coming. Or, in a different series, his team winning and telling him how much he had missed out on.

When he finally woke up, it was 11:37 am, in the local time of Pune, Maharashtra. He yawned and blinked. There was light streaming through the curtains. His mom was telling him to get ready, and he wore a vibrant orange kurta.

They walked down the street to the colony's Ganpati Idol, a statue 4 feet tall of the god with an elephant head. There were red hibiscus flowers all over, Ganpati's favorite, and everywhere the Ganpati was wheeled around, there were big drums and cymbals called Dhol Tasha preceding and following it. After the puja, or prayer ceremony, everyone got to eat a dessert called Modak, a dumpling with a filling of coconut and jaggery shaped like a closed rose bud, to celebrate. Later, kids performed in a talent show, singing and dancing to famous Bollywood songs. It was jam packed and full of bright, colorful kurtas, saris, turbans, flowers, and much more. It was loud, almost like a mob at a concert. Everybody was yelling, "Ganpati Bappa Morya!", meaning 'Long Live Ganpati'.

As the festival progressed over the next few days, Aadi felt his attitude change. He learned about Ganpati, met lots of distant relatives that he'd never met before, and even heard a bunch of folktales! At the end, Aadi was extremely glad his parents had pushed him to come to "The Oxford of the East" or "The Learning Capital of India", where the excitement was palpable. Everybody also started to say 'come back next year, Lord Ganpati, in Marathi, and both Kavya and Aadi were amazed at the energy levels.

When he got back home, he texted his teammates and found out that they had won. But it didn't feel like he had missed out. He was grateful he had gone to Pune and learned about his culture, the festival, and even his name, which was inspired by Ganpati! It was the experience of a lifetime. Before, his eyes only noticed soccer balls, but now he was opening up to hibiscuses around him.

ABOUT THE AUTHOR

Riyan Onkar is 11 years old and loves sports, reading, and playing guitar. He dreams of becoming a professional soccer player someday. He wants all kids to be good human beings, be responsible, and prioritize their education.

Chapter 4

The Diwali Festival Debate

As I walked into the school halls, I was surprised to see not only one, but two new flyers presented on the board, and both of them were about Diwali. I guess it's reasonable that these flyers are up, I mean the festival is practically right around the corner. As I checked the timings for both festivals, a light bulb burst into my head. I got my phone out and posted a debate on the school board. Well, I guess this'll be fun.

The first few hours of school flew by in a heartbeat, and before I knew it, lunch began. I sat down with my friends as they asked about the thing

I posted on the school web. "Hey Saarth, is it true that there's going to be a competition between both of the new Diwali festivals?" one of my friends asked. "Yup, I'll be attending both of them and will be writing an article about each one. Then, the school will decide who the winner is on its own," I replied. Both festivals are on Saturday, but are prepared on different timings, so it's possible for me to host this debate. For the rest of the school day, I'm lost in thought for what both festivals will bring to their table. The festivals were 3 days from now, but even so, for those next few days, I was only thinking about the parties, until it was the day itself.

"Beep, Beep," was the sound of my alarm clock on the morning of the big day. I brushed my teeth, changed into my t-shirt, and was off to the super market to buy treats for the festivals. For the North Indian festival, we were instructed to bring at least 20 sweets of the same kind, which is what I'm doing as we speak. I wonder, what will they use all of these sweets for?

I checked the time from my watch, and saw that there was only 10 minutes till the first festival. As I decorated the treats with raping paper, I hopped back into my car and made my way to the school. The North Indian Diwali celebration was first, and when I got there, I dashed out of my car with my notebook in hand. Once I started to see the school's front door, I placed my ID onto the scanner and made myself welcome to the school halls.

The poster said that the North Indian Diwali festival would be held in room 205, so that is where I went. I took a left, went upstairs, and there I saw the door wide open, as if it was waiting for me to arrive.

The front door was decorated with a rangoli, and a few diyas on the sides of the door. Well, that's a beautiful sight to see. I walked into the room, and was immediately greeted with people saying 'Happy Diwali' all around. I, first, gave one of the sweet boxes I bought to the host of the celebration, and she immediately thanked me in reply. After I exchanged greetings with everyone at the party, it was only when the party had started to commence.

We first played a handful of games, traditional ones that included Carrom, Bambaram, and more. We even played a few worldwide games, such as Ludo and Chess, though these 2 games were in fact first made by India. The next thing that was on our list was reading books that talked about how Diwali in Northern India was celebrated. Such as how they usually celebrated the holiday for 5 days, and how they did poojas for the goddess Lekshmi. Though on the last page of the book, it stated how they exchanged gifts, which is what we started to do right after reading it. All 20 of us started to exchange gifts that each of us brought or made, and in the end I had 10 new things filled up in my hands. Well, I have to say that the Northern Indian festival sure was a blast, so I do wonder how the Southern festival will get their upper hand.

It's not supposed to start until an hour and half, so I went back into my car and started writing about the Northern Indian festival. Who knows, maybe I can finish this article in the car itself. While I was writing, I completely lost track of time, and realized it was only 5 minutes until the next festival started. I sprang from my car seat and made my way to the track. I was told that this would be where the Southern festival would be held, and when I got there, I was not disappointed.

There were 5 tables of snacks, with chairs on the side of them. Similarly to the Northern Indian festival, there were also rangoli and diyas. Though what really made me excited was the box of fireworks, just sitting there and ready to be ignited. Once the clock hit 7:45, we all were allowed to take the fireworks. I grabbed some of them at random, and what I saw in my hands was a bit disappointing. I only grabbed the smaller ones, but hey, at least I get to see the bigger ones in action. As I ignited the fireworks I had, I saw in awe that some of the bigger ones reached the tops of the sky. Wow, just wow. As we wrapped up all of the fireworks, we started to eat the dishes that were offered to us. There were naans, biryanis, and more. Honestly, all the food just looked so good, that I had to try each one. Of course I couldn't finish it all, so on my way home I took the leftover food with me. Gosh this day was a blast. I do wonder who will be the winner though.

When the next day arrived, I completed both of the articles and posted them on the school board. I emphasized on what both teams had to offer, and waited for the school to decide who the final winner would be. The post would be on for about 3 days, and as usual I still couldn't get my mind off of the post.

I checked it every hour, and saw the leaderboard change every time. Then finally, when the moment arrived, the 3 days were over, and I was standing on the school stage as the representatives of both festivals waited anxiously.

I first introduced myself and the festival while reading both articles. Then I let the guests get some food before I announced the winner, and finally the moment everyone was waiting for. When I was about to tell the school who won the festival, I was both shocked and happy with the results.

I cleared my throat as I announced, "The winner of the Diwali festival is... both of the teams! This year's Diwali festival has resulted in a tie!" Everyone clapped in awe, and saw that both groups were pleased by the results, and we continued having a blast at the party.

I guess sometimes fate itself has its own way of telling us that both festivals are unique in their own way, and they both deserve the right to win.

ABOUT THE AUTHOR

Saravana Ranga is 12 years old and loves biking, reading, and playing the violin. She dreams of becoming a medical technologist someday. She wants for there to be no harsh comparisons between others and for people to respect others by who they are.

Chapter 5

Parth's Promise

No one dared to stand up against the bullies of Minnesota Elementary School, except Parth. Mark and Justin were the two guys everyone feared. They are both in the 3rd grade but they often made fun of other kids. If they saw someone different or unique they would laugh and call them names.

Sarah is a 8-year-old girl with long black hair and wears traditional Indian clothes. She has a thick Indian accent and brings her mom's home cooked meals for lunch. For other kids this makes her special, but for Mark and Justin she is the prime candidate for their antics. One Friday at school, they cornered Sarah and started hitting her. She pleaded for them to stop and wailed for help. Her pleas fell on deaf ears with Mark and Justin. Sarah's brother was watching from one class over. Afraid to intervene, Parth stood there in fear wanting to help his beloved sister. Eventually Mark and Justin became bored and headed back to their classroom.

Sarah's face was battered and bruised from the punches they threw at her. She was hurt but she couldn't do anything. In desperation she told their teacher but she refused to take action. Their teacher was Mark's mom. Sarah shamefully walked back to her classroom, silently pleading for this to end. Her classmates could see the marks on her face, but not one person wanted to get on Mark and Justin's bad side. At home their mom asks Sarah why her face is bruised. She lies not wanting to get targeted even more by the bullies.

In the evening, the wind screams and wails. Parth's family celebrates Rama Navami to commemorate the heroic deeds of lord Rama. Parth learns about his dedication to protecting his wife Sira from the forces of evil. That night Parth lays on his comfortable mattress and thinks about how he wants to protect Sarah just like how Rama protects Sira. Parth wakes up still unsure on how to help Sarah. At school the bullies once again beat Sarah up, this time

Parth takes a step forward and confronts the bullies. Mark and Justin look at Parth with malice that causes Parth to back off.

Sarah screams," Help me!"

Parth strolls back to class, defeated and sorrowful. During lunch Sarah sits alone in the cafeteria eating the butter chicken and naan her mom packed.

Mark exclaims," What is that awful smell!"

The students begin to snicker and make remarks about Sarah's lunch. Sarah watches as her peers all laugh at her traditional lunch. Parth notices the neutral expression on Sarah's face turn to a gloomy frown. Tears silently falling and Sarah's cheek turning a shade of bright red. Sarah prays for this moment of pure embarrassment to end. She hopes that this event will become an afterthought lost in the back of everyone's mind. Never to be brought up again.

Later in the final class of the day, Mrs. Hannah asks Sarah to solve a math equation.

"She poses a question," What is one hundred divided by 5?"

"Twenty-five", she answers.

"No that is incorrect", Mrs Hannah explains.

The class explodes into ruckus laughter after she gets the question wrong.

Justin exclaims, "Aren't Indians supposed to be smart?"

At home, Parth discusses the issue with his mom and dad. They say they have tried to get it to stop but the principal won't take action on them.

Parth's mom says," She needs you to protect her." "Show those bullies that they can't mess with your sister!"

Parth lies down on his white cot, thinking...

At school, Mark and Justin start hurting Sarah again, throwing insults left and right. Parth marches toward them, anger swelling up in his eyes. He looks them dead in the eye.

"Leave her alone", he says.

His glare intimidates them, like a tiger hunting its prey.

"If you mess with her again you'll have to go through me", he says with a bellowing voice.

The bullies sprint away as fast as a cheetah. Sarah embraces Parth with the warmest hug imaginable.

"Thank you", she mutters.

Lunch time rolls around and Sarah expects to be tormented. Her peers huddle beside her and ask about her culture, this time with good intent. She is thrilled.

In the evening, Sarah thanks Parth profusely. She is finally free from her bullies. Parth is glad for his sister.

Being unique is what makes us who we are, so embrace everyone's differences with curiosity.

Diya Patel is 12 years old and enjoys singing, dancing, and soccer. She dreams of becoming a doctor to follow her dad's footsteps. She wants all kids to follow their dreams even if someone tells them they can't do it.

Chapter 6

Holi Chaos

Manoj was that one kid in his group of friends that likes to watch Holi from his balcony for safety and away from chaos. But one day in the 2 days of Holi his friend carried him from his arms and legs and took him to play Holi. But he was pushing, protesting and even threatening his friends but they kept moving until finally they got there.

By the time they let him go they were already miles away from his apartment so there was no turning back. On top of that they even said, "If you're a boy you will play".

It was time for bonfire, when Manoj went to throw his clothes in it he was pushed in but fortunately only his hand went in and got burned he was in so much pain and the fire was melting the poop on him and the pink was completely gone, he rushed to cold water and he turned out to be okay.

It stung his eyes like a hundred tiny needles. He rubbed them furiously, but that only made the burn worse. His friends led him to a tap, where he splashed water until he could see again—though everything still looked a little pink. He could finally look at the hot and shining sun because the pink blocks out the rays of the sun.

While he was trying to book an uber to get home a person body slammed him and sent him flying across the field and landed in a pile of animal poop. When he finally got back up his brother ran to him to make sure he did not get hurt. His brother helped him book an uber and he went straight to the massage studio to get a massage and that got a lot of the pain out physically

Although he was moaning and groaning as he looked back, he realized he had a pretty nice time not including the accidents. So next he is coming back for more.

ABOUT THE AUTHOR

Sharan Chulani is an 11-year-old. He enjoys Tennis and helping people. He hopes that everyone knows that time is an important part of our lives.

Chapter 7

Pere Noel's best Christmas

Hooray, Christmas is almost here! It's the best holiday season because we get gifts and there are colorful parades. Hi, I'm Simon from the beautiful French countryside.

Well, every year in our neighborhood, the Christmas father named Père Noël goes down people's chimneys and places the gifts in the fireplace and the Christmas trees. This is a tradition in France and so I have decided to be the Père Noël this year. So, I went to the store to check what gifts I could get for my Neighbors.

I saw a cooking set for Laura, who loves cooking Italian food. Next was a kid named Matthew, who considered video games his favorite hobby, so I bought him a video game console. Then there was an old man beside the park in our community named Albert who wished for a new glass, so I bought him a pair of - glasses for his blonde brown eyes. Finally, there was Luke, a first-grader who loves soccer, so I bought him a Soccer Table. I went home that evening, packed the gifts, ate dinner, and went to church for the Christmas vigil.

After coming home, I went to the charcoal-coated chimneys of my friends and placed the gifts in the fireplace, and went back home to sleep. The next day was Christmas Day. I went to visit my friends to share my wishes and asked about the gifts. But they said, "Oh, that's so kind of you, but it's not there ".

So, I asked the other friend, and she said I saw a shadow of the mysterious little human in a red hoodie, packing the gifts in a bag like a robber.

While we were speaking about it, our old friend Albert said, "I'm a retired policeman and I will investigate.

During his investigation, he found that the little creature is a little girl from the nearby community. Albert said, "I could find near the chimneys, many tiny woolen threads from the red hoodie the girl was wearing. It is none other than Lia, who is timid and jealous that she doesn't have any friends to be with."

We all met her, and I asked, "Did you steal the gifts?".

She said, "Yeah, I saw you buying gifts in the store, and you dropped the paper which has a list of gifts for people in the store. "I looked at it and it made me feel jealous, so I stole the gifts as I don't know any Pere Noel to share Christmas gifts with me,"

She cried. We all felt bad for her and decided to gift her a bright red dress for Christmas. We also invited her for the Christmas lunch which consists of authentic delicious Christmas French food like Lobster Thermidor with Caviar, Green Beans etc.

Lia was very happy and felt sorry for stealing the gifts. She cried out again and said, "Thank you so much for forgiving me and accepting me as your friend".

This is the best Christmas ever in my life as Pere Noel.

ABOUT THE AUTHOR

Raphael Bernie, a 9-year-old with a passion for painting, creative arts, story writing, and outdoor play with friends, has a deep interest in teaching and hopes to share his favorite subjects with others in the future. He believes that even a few minutes of focused reading each day can make a meaningful contribution to building strong reading habits.

Chapter 8

Ranabhasini

Once there was a girl who died in a car accident. After one year of being dead, God found a good soul in her, then they finally figured that they needed a child Goddess on the Earth so they could learn more about the humans and provide them with a lot of resources. To bring her back in this human life, the Supreme Gods, Brahma, Vishnu and Shivan did the act of courage and narrated "Om!" about seven times.

Then the human Goddess was born. Vishnu took the form of Matsya Avatar, again to bring her to the Earth!!

Once she arrived on earth, she was found on the shores of Kerala. Then a family found her and her parents named her Ranabhasini.

As she grew, she started to get the blessings from the Gods. Hanuman gave her a tail. Ganesha gave her a Trunk. The Tail and Trunk got attached to her body. Then Durga gave her a Lion, Shiva gave her a Crescent, which gets attached to her head. Karthikeya gave her a Peacock.

No matter how she looked, her parents loved her dearly!!!

She was homeschooled in the past years, then her parents decided that she needed some friends, so they sent her to school.

On the first day of school in the morning. Her mother worked her up and said, "Sweetheart! You must get ready for your first day of school. I think you will make a lot of friends "

When her dad was dropping her to school, she saw the whole school building. It was three times the size of her house! Then the school bell rang!

Her father said, "Have a nice day on the first day of school!" She spirited away to her school.

There was one problem. She did not know which classroom she was in. Then her teacher Ms. Chandu Bai said, "Hello! happy to see you. Are you new to the school?"

Ranabhasini replied, "Yes I am new to the school, and my name is Ranabhasini."

Ms. Chandu Bai said, "Oh! you are in my class. Come, I will show you around our classroom." When she entered her class, she saw a boy named Mandy. He said "Oh! you look so ugly!!".

Then Ms. Chandu Bai said, "Don't be so harsh. Do you want me to put you in timeout?"

He said "Sorry, Ranabhasini", then it was almost time to start the class. Her teacher escorted Ranabhasini to her table.

She sat with a few kids named Tamara, Kumar, Ravi and Sana. Once she sat down, the teacher started explaining about the subject and predicate.

Then the bell rang for recess.

Ms. Chandu Bai said, "Already class is over? Time passes quickly!" Then the kids went out for recess. Ranabhasini started playing with Sana, she asked, "Would you mind if I ask about something?" Ranabhasini said, "Go, ahead!"

Sana said, "Why do you have an elephant trunk?" Ranabhasini said.

"I don't know but my mom says, it's a blessing from God!"

Sana said "Oh, my gosh! it's so, so, crazy. You might even become popular".

Then Ranabhasini asked, "Do you know who Mandy is?"

Sana said "You mean Mandy!? Mandy is 100% mean! One time he called me a loser, when I lost a game! So technically he's so mean! just stay away from him."

Ranabhasini said "OK."

Then the bell rang for lunchtime. Once everybody came to the lunch table, they opened what they brought out for lunch. Ravi had spicy noodles for lunch with ketchup. Sana had brought fried chicken. Ranabhasini brought the best lunch, dosa!

Mandy who was two seats away said, "Dosa! It's old school. What about Gobi Manchurian?"

Tamara said, "Stop making fun of Ranabhasini. It's just her first day of school!"

Then Mandy said, "I don't care, you know my mom owns the school!"

Ranabhasini asked, "What does he mean?"

Ravi said "Well, his mom is the principal of the school."

Mandy anxiously said "Well, yeah!!"

Then a girl came next Monday. Ranabhasini asked, "Who was that girl?"

Sana said, "Oh it's Mandy's sister, named Reena. They are twins!"

Reena asked Mandy, "Where is mom? I can't find her."

Mandy said, "I don't know."

Then the bell rang, it was time for Math class. They were given a packet of problems. Kids started to solve the math questions by then, the bell rang, and school was over.

Once Ranabhasini came home, she sat next to her lion and peacock petting them both then a loud sound came near her house entrance.

Hiss! Hiss! There was the sound. She sought towards the direction of the sound in the playground near her home, her nemesis Mandy was in danger. He was screaming!

There was an anaconda near Mandy, trying to attack him. Ranabhasini realized that it was Lord Shiva, so she decided to help Mandy. She peacefully spoke to Lord Shiva, not to hurt Mandy. Lord Shiva spoke to Mandy, "You should not bully anyone based on their looks. It's cruel to do that. That is a lesson for you today!"

He guided Ranabhasini to the sky and showed her the Supreme Gods. God blessed Ranabhasini and sent her back to Earth, she happily lived with her family and friends!

ABOUT THE AUTHOR

Vanessa Zoe D Ranjith, is 9 year old and enjoys drawing, reading books, playing chess & is an avid learner of Piano. She dreams of inventing devices / findings which can create differences for humans. She reminds kids to be kind and be inclusive with their peers around!

Chapter 9

Riddles for Runners

On a quiet day, under the ordinary world we all know of, lies a fantasy world where skyscrapers stand tall and creatures of all kinds roam without trouble, twelve-year-old Vik Malhotra was no ordinary kid.

Vik worked at his uncle's shop, Oddly Fast. He was called a Runner, delivering magical items all over the city. He'd delivered just about everything, from collars that made your dog talk to glasses that could see the truth.

But today, he had received something he'd never delivered before. A backpack his uncle handed it to him, seriously. "Don't open it, and don't talk to it"

Vik cocked his head. "Talk to.... what?"

But his uncle had disappeared. Probably to feed his singing plants. Vik sighed, slinging the bag over his shoulders. As he looked over his route, he noticed his route would take him across the entire city, to a library called The Archive. Vik immediately recognized the name. The Archive belonged to his uncle's friend, and he remembered how much he was a help to his uncle. He put on a determined expression, and started his journey halfway through, everything had been going well, until the backpack moved.

Then, a ghostly figure flew out of the backpack, grinning down at Vik. "Betaal's the name, riddles are my kind of game!" He explained, spinning around Vik, who stood shocked.

Betaal rolled his eyes at Vik, annoyed. "I know, I know you aren't supposed to speak to me unless we get to the archive. But I'm bored, so it's time for a riddle!"

Vik stayed silent and started to walk again.

Betaal zoomed next to him. "Here's your first one!"

"A rich man gives away all his money and is called wise. A poor man gives his last coin and is called foolish. Who gave more?"

Vik mumbled. "The poor man" without thinking.

Poof! Betaal vanished, and Vik groaned.

He'd have to start over.

After he traveled back to retrieve the bag (and also to get a scolding from his uncle), Vik continued walking.

Betaal took this as an opportunity, "You see your best friend steal something to help her hungry family. If you tell, she'll be punished. If you don't, you're helping her steal. What do you do?"

Vik stayed silent against his own will, continuing to walk.

Betaal frowned, sighing. "I thought I would get you on that one."

By the time they had reached the street of the library, Betaal tried again.

"A dragon guards two eggs.

One will hatch into a monster.

One into a hero.

You can only save one.

Which one do you choose?"

Vik furrowed his eyebrows. He didn't know. Maybe there wasn't an answer. Nonetheless, he stayed silent.

At last, the Archive came into view, the towering building glowing in blue light. Betaal follows Vik into the building, quiet.

"You really stayed silent. You win" he said, smiling softly at Vik. "But did you learn anything?"

Vik almost spoke again but pulled out a notepad. He wrote on the paper and gave it to Betaal with a big smile.

"Your riddles aren't just riddles. They are choices, choices we decide to make that make the future, just like in real life." Then without answering Vik kept writing, "If you help a person to do wrong, to do a greater good, it's not always wrong. But if it's your job to guard something, then it doesn't matter if they are going to do right or wrong, you have to perform your duty no matter what."

Betaal nodded. "That's what I wanted to show. I asked a thousand kings and warriors over the years, and none learned from them. They only wanted to be right."

He started to walk off. "Tell this story well, Vik, and who knows, maybe we'll meet again." And with that, he disappeared.

Vik stared at the backpack, and inside there was a glowing notebook, in the same glowing blue.

In the first page, it read:

"RIDDLES FOR RUNNERS

Use wisely. Tell bravely.

Speak when ready."

Vik smiled.

With this book, he may not be the fastest to answer, but he would teach others sometimes it's best to stop, and think.

ABOUT THE AUTHOR

Sahana is a 13-year-old who loves listening to music, dancing to her heart and be expressive through drawing. She dreams of becoming a psychologist. She wants all kids to know, when you read, try and understand the meaning of whatever the story is telling you.

Chapter 10

A Light to New Friendship

Meera carefully sprinkled the colored sand in the shape of a beautiful flower. Meera missed India, the Diwali celebration there was one of a kind! She got yellow sand and made a symmetrical flower next to her first one.

She remembered how her cousins had taught her how to make beautiful rangoli which is also known as colored sand. She was about to go inside to get lamps (diyas) when she heard a step behind her.

Meera turned around and saw a girl.

"Hi!" She said, "I'm Neva, I'm your new neighbor. What are you doing?" She asked but not meanly.

"Rangoli." Meera said, "It's a part of Diwali."

"Huh? What's that?" Neva asked.

"It's a holiday my mom told me this story of Diwali, now I know I can tell you how we celebrate it.

"Sure." Neva said.

Meera smiled and took a deep breath and began. "Once upon a time long, long ago there was a prince named Ram, Ram had a brother named Lakshman and a wife named Sita. Ram had to go into exile for fourteen years because his father had asked him.

The trio agreed and eventually found a place to settle down in the deep forest. There was a beautiful creek with birds, flowers and animals. One day while Ram and Lakshman were away an evil king named Ravan with ten heads, and twenty arms came disguised as a poor traveler. Ram had told Sita not to open the door to anyone at all.

Sita had obeyed and was doing housework. Ravan knocked on the door. I'm a hungry old man. Please let me in. Sita was kind and had a big heart, so she opened the door but the minute she did, Ravan turned into his true form. And captured Sita and took her to his castle on his flying chariot, which was in Lanka, an island across the Indian ocean.

Luckily, Sita was smart, she dropped the beads of her necklace leaving a trail for Ram to find. Ram and Lakshman returned shortly, Ram saw the beads and recognized them as Sita's; he followed the trail, and it led him to Hanuman the Monkey God.

They continued to follow the beads until they came to a giant ocean the Indian Ocean. There was no way to get across, Hanuman called his team of monkeys, and they decided to make a bridge with stones but to prevent them from sinking they wrote the word "Ram" and then the rocks floated. Once the bridge was done, they crossed over it and arrived in Lanka.

A ginormous battle happened with Ravan's forces and Ram, Hanuman, Lakshman and all the monkeys. The battle lasted many weeks, but at last

Ram pulled out a special arrow and shot all of Ravan's heads at the same time. They had won!

Sita, Ram and Lakshman happily started the journey back home. And to show them the way people lit oil lamps called diyas and made beautiful patterns on their porches with Rangoli to welcome them home. And that is the story of Diwali," Meera proudly finished.

Nowadays, people celebrate Diwali by making Rangoli, lighting oil lamps, decorating their houses, praying and making delicious Indian sweets.

"Wow!" Neva said, "That's so cool. Do you think I could help? "

"Sure" Meera answered happily, Meera taught Neva how to make Rangoli and light diyas (they also ate a lot of Indian sweets).

"Diwali is super fun" Neva announced and after that day the two friends always celebrated Diwali together.

ABOUT THE AUTHOR

Yashvi Gandhi is a 10-year-old who has a passion for reading, writing, gymnastics, and playing the piano. She also loves spending time outdoors, exploring nature and enjoying fresh air. Yashvi dreams of becoming an author one day, as she believes that words are a powerful way to express thoughts and emotions. Through her love for writing, she hopes to inspire others and make a positive impact. Her message to all children is: "Follow your dreams. Nothing is too difficult if you keep practicing and never give up.

Chapter 11

The Two Houses

I was sprinting across the soccer field, mud flying everywhere, because something AMAZING had just happened. "Come on! You've gotta see this!" I yelled, nearly tripping over my untied shoelace.

Here's the deal: every year, our town has this giant Easter egg hunt. And not just any egg hunt. The mayor hides ONE golden egg. Whoever finds it gets free ice cream for the whole summer. Basically, it's like winning the lottery, but better.

This year, my friend Jordan found the egg first. He held it up like a superhero. "I win! Free ice cream FOREVER!" Everyone groaned, because, well,

Jordan is the kind of guy who eats ice cream in front of you and says, "Too bad you don't have any."

But then—disaster. He tripped, dropped the egg, and it rolled right into the storm drain. *Plop.* Gone. Vanished. Bye-bye forever.

Everyone groaned louder. "Guess there's no prize this year," someone muttered. Jordan sat down in the mud and said, "This is the worst day of my life." (Which is a little dramatic if you ask me, but still.)

For the next three days, nobody even talked about the egg. It was like it had never existed.

But then—plot twist! On the morning of the third day, the golden egg showed up again. Not in the storm drain. Not cracked in half. Just sitting there, shiny as the sun, right in the middle of the playground slide.

The kids screamed. People pointed. One kid fainted into the mulch (okay, maybe that was just drama). And then we all cheered like crazy. The egg was BACK.

Nobody knew how. Nobody cared. What mattered was this: just when we thought the story was over, it wasn't. There was hope again. There was ice cream again!

ABOUT THE AUTHOR

Jonah Mascarenhas is nine years old and loves to read, play basketball and tennis. When he is older, he wants to become a sports newscaster. All kids should always do activities to be healthy.

Chapter 12

Saving Diwali

On a very colorful day, there was a girl named Ishita. Ishita and her mom were decorating the house for Diwali with lights and colors. While Ishita was doing the lights, her mom was cooking food for the guest who will come over. All the guests who were coming to the party were going to come at 7 pm and the girls were going to wear a sari.

After Ishita's mom was done cooking the delicious food, she now had to decorate the gods. She used colorful flowers, fruits, and more. It was almost time for the party, so Ishita and her mom were going to get ready.

While Ishita's dad was in the basement, he was looking for the fireworks. He could not find it, so he checked one more time. Then he realized he forgot to buy it. He told Ishita and Ishita's mom. They were shocked.

Ishita's dad was trying to think of a plan or else they can't do the fireworks. Then a knock came from the door. It was their neighbor. Ishita panicked! She did not know what to do. Then her dad came up with an idea. He decided to go to the local market. When he got there, he could not find any, so he asked an employee. The employee said they ran out of fireworks.

Ishita's dad went home, worried about what to do. After a few minutes Ishita had a plan to go to the neighbor's house and ask them, so she went, and they had extra. Then Ishita took the extra and celebrated with the fireworks. All Ishita's friends were happy that the best part of Diwali was happening and thanked her.

ABOUT THE AUTHOR

Shrinika Rajapuram is 10 years old. She enjoys soccer, gymnastics, and volleyball. She wants to become a pro gymnast. One advice she would give to the kids who are reading is to work hard to become a better person.

Chapter 13

The Blessed Distraction

It was a beautiful day in Los Angeles, California. It is Anthony's birthday. Jack, Anthony's younger brother, who sees Anthony like a god, gave Anthony a present. "OH MY GOD- JACK, IS THIS THE MBA24K VIDEO GAME?!?!?!"

Anthony nods. "Yup, I spent all of my tooth fairy money on that. Heard you talking about that with your friends."

"That is so sweet" thought Anthony, *I must get him something awesome too.*

A few days later, Jack was walking home from school, when Anthony met him at the door.

"Hi, Anthony, what's up?" Jack said.

Anthony gave him the bag and said nothing.

"Wow! A catapult! This is going to be fun. Thanks bro!" Jack said devilishly.

How little it takes to make that kid's day. Anthony said to himself, *that makes me feel good.*

Anthony walks home to find Jack filling up water balloons. "Waycha doing?" Anthony said.

"Nothing." Jack said, winking. *I got him a video game, and he got me this catapult. I'll show him!*

Anthony, confused, left to go to his friend and neighbor's house. Raj moved from India to LA when he was five, so, they still celebrated many Indian holidays, like Diwali and Ganesh Chaturthi together. Every year they enjoyed lighting candles and making the little elephant god with bio degradable clay.

They started talking about different holidays they were going to celebrate this year, as Ganesh Chaturthi was around the corner, when Raj heard a knock at the door. They both got up to answer it, when the door swung open to reveal Jack with the catapult, and a full arsenal of water balloons.

"Hey Anthony." Jack said, "JACK. YOU. ARE. DEAD."

SPLAT!!!

The water balloons hit Anthony, hard. Anthony was in shock and began to run.

Jack began to chase him into Raj's backyard. He kept hitting him with water balloons, that hurt badly.

"AAAAAA! AAAA! Stop Jack, I gave that to you!" Anthony screamed.

"MWAHAHA!!!" Jack laughed as he pelted Anthony with balloons. Neighborhood doors swung open hearing the screams. Some of the kids began laughing and recording the chaos.

Anthony made it inside his house before he got completely soaked. Jack sat down at the top of a hill, waiting for Anthony to come out. His plan was when Anthony stepped out, he'd open fire on him and really get him.

Raj walked up the hill to Jack, and said, "You know if you fire it backwards, it will hit harder?"

"Really?" Jack asked.

"Yup, try it out." Raj replied. Raj pulled at the catapult outside instead of towards himself and let go. BAM! He shot HIMSELF!

"Hahaha!" Anthony laughed, he was watching from the window. "Looks like you got a taste of his own medicine." Anthony said as he walked outside.

Raj said, "This has kind of become the story of Bhasmaasura."

"Huh?" Jack and Anthony said.

"Ugh, I guess I have to tell you now, don't I?"

Jack and Anthony nodded innocently.

Raj sat down and the boys sat in front of him, "The Bhasmasura story is a Hindu mythological where a demon, after performing penance, receives a boon from Lord Shiva to turn anyone into ashes by touching their head. Intending to use this power on Shiva…"

Anthony chimed in, " Dang, using the power given to you ON the person who gave it to you, that's messed up." He looked pointedly at his younger brother Jack, who ignored him with an eye roll.

"Sounds familiar?" Raj asked. But before they could answer he continued. "The demon is then tricked by Lord Vishnu disguised as the beautiful dancer Mohini. During a dance, Mohini makes a gesture that Bhasmasura imitates, touching his own head and instantly turning himself into ashes."

Jack laughed, "That is cruel, but he deserved it."

Just then, Jack and Anthony's mom called them, and they ran down the hill, to go home.

"Oy, they still don't get it, do they?" Raj said to his dog who was wagging his tail joyfully. "Wurf!"

"Yeah, I didn't think so." Raj looked at the catapult next to him and picked it up to take them to their home, to hide them from Jack.

ABOUT THE AUTHOR

Sharvi Singh is an 11 year old who enjoys baking, making up songs and creating new things. She dreams of becoming a baker or entrepreneur. Every child should know that they are unique in the way they are and how they look.

About The
Coach and Editor

Aditi Wardhan Singh is an author, coach, and founder of RaisingWorldChildren.com, a platform dedicated to empowering multicultural families. With expertise in cultural sensitivity, bilingualism, and third-culture experiences, she helps parents and educators raise globally aware, confident children. Aditi's journey growing up between cultures informs her work, making her a passionate advocate for cultural awareness and inclusivity. As an accomplished writer, her books and articles focus on identity, belonging, and resilience, offering guidance on overcoming cultural challenges and fostering empathy in children.

With over 14 books written and 3 in the works, her book is an effort to encourage the next generation to be accomplished writers, understand publishing, and be critical thinkers about culture and belonging.

If you are interested in submitting your child's writing for publication in Write to Publish program, email - contact@raisingworldchildren.com